D0952905

'Tis a very old wish
And I've sent it before
But my
"Merry Christmas"
Never meant more

To_____

Merry Christmas
From

Also by
Barbara Milo Ohrbach

Merry Christmas

BY
BARBARA MILO OHRBACH

❄ ❄ ❄

*Festive Stories, Songs, Poems,
Recipes, and Gift Ideas
for the Holidays*

CLARKSON POTTER/PUBLISHERS
NEW YORK

Every effort has been made to locate the copyright holders of materials used in this book. Should there be any omissions or errors, we apologize and shall be pleased to make the appropriate acknowledgments in future editions.

Grateful acknowledgment is made to the following for permission to reprint previously published material: Lord & Taylor Christmas Institutional, © 1990, reprinted with gracious permission from Lord & Taylor. Extract from "The Everlasting Mercy," 1911 by John Masefield. Acknowledgment is made to The Society of Authors as the literary representative of the Estate of John Masefield. "Under the Mistletoe" from *Copper Sun*, by Countee Cullen, © 1927 by Harper & Brothers: copyright renewed 1955 by Ida M. Cullen. Reprinted by permission of GRM Associates, Agents for the Estate of Ida M. Cullen.

Published by Clarkson Potter/Publishers, 201 East 50th Street, New York, New York 10022. Member of the Crown Publishing Group.

CLARKSON N. POTTER, POTTER and colophon are trademarks of Clarkson N. Potter, Inc.

Manufactured in Japan

Design by Justine Strasberg
Calligraphy by Tim Girvin

Library of Congress Cataloging-in-Publication Data
Merry Christmas/[compiled] by Barbara Milo Ohrbach.
p.   cm.
"Festive stories, songs, poems, recipes, and gift ideas for the holidays."
1. Christmas—Literary collections.   2. Christmas cookery.
3. Carols.   I. Ohrbach, Barbara Milo.
PN6071.C6M45
808.8'033—dc20   91-12882
                                                                              CIP

ISBN: 0-517-58626-6

10   9   8   7   6   5   4   3   2   1

First Edition

Joyous Christmas

Table of Contents

Affectionate thank-yous and merry wishes to all who worked on this little book: Beth Allen, Gayle Benderoff, Martina D'Alton, Lisa Fresne, Deborah Geltman, Vie and Al Koerner, Patti McCarthy, Mel Ohrbach, Camille Prehatney, Rita and Harry Singer, Carol Southern, Tina Strasberg, Gerry Tandy, and Shirley Wohl. Particular gratitude to everyone at my publishers for their contributions: María Bottino, Cathy Collins, Allan Eady, David Eiland, Phyllis Fleiss, Jonathan Fox, Chip Gibson, Barbara Kantor, Lisa Keim, Howard Klein, Barbara Marks, Matthew Mayer, Bill Nave, Teresa Nicholas, Ed Otto, Pam Romano, Robin Strashun, Michelle Sidrane, Jane Treuhaft, and Helen Zimmermann.

Introduction

They were not a handsome family; they were not well dressed; their shoes were far from being waterproof; their clothes were scanty; and Peter might have known, and very likely did, the inside of a pawnbroker's. But they were happy, grateful, pleased with one another, and contented with the time.

CHARLES DICKENS

Like most children, I was never more "contented with the time" than at Christmas. It was a time filled with anticipation, and I was never disappointed.

Each year, our tree was hung with the same ornaments. It was fun to read the ads from earlier Christmases as each fragile object was carefully unpacked from its nest of yellowing newspapers. I still have my favorite ornament, an iridescent glass swan, which managed to remain intact from one Christmas to the next.

Our whole family was always together during the holidays. My beloved grandparents were the first to arrive on Christmas morning, loaded down with packages, and with lots of kisses. Grandma, as she did every year, would head straight for the kitchen. Grandpa, who loved playing practical jokes, would wander around the house in search of an unsuspecting victim, preferably one under ten years old! I still remember some of the presents I received then: a shiny red scooter, a patent hatbox for ballet, an armoire made by my father for my Ginny doll's clothes.

As we get older, I think it's important to preserve the connection with the magic times we remember. To me, Christmas really means tradition and heartfelt associations. All of us, at one time or another during the bustle of the holidays, may forget that Christmas, after all, celebrates a very simple story; and it's the simple things that remain and take on greater significance.

In this little stocking stuffer I've gathered together some wonderful poems and stories that are part of the fabric of the season—such as Teddy Roosevelt's letter to his children and Winston Churchill's remarks on his Christmas in America during World War II. I hope you'll like the sweet Victorian Christmas cards and ornaments that illustrate each page. Included also are some simple recipes for favorite holiday classics. I like to have tasty treats on hand for unexpected guests. Some also make delicious gifts for those near and far.

In 1875, Washington Irving wrote: "The world has become more worldly; . . . it has lost many of its local peculiarities, its home-bred feelings, its fireside delights." Over a century later, I couldn't agree more. What do I really want for Christmas this year? That's easy—the simple, warm, contented feeling I had when I was eight years old.

Barbara Milo Ohrbach
New York

Christmas is a spontaneous drama of the common folk, a prayer, a hymn. All the while that Raphael was painting the Sistine Madonna, Frenchmen building the cathedral of Chartres, English bishops composing the Book of Common Prayer, Handel his Messiah, Bach his B-Minor Mass, the common people, out of whom these geniuses sprang, were composing Christmas.

DR. EARL COUNT

Not believe in Santa Claus! You might as well not believe in fairies. . . . Yes, Virginia, there is a Santa Claus. He exists as certainly as love and generosity and devotion exist.

FRANCIS P. CHURCH

It is more blessed to give than to receive.

ACTS

Glorious Fruitcake Gifts

In A Christmas Memory Truman Capote writes: "A morning arrives in November, and my friend, as though officially inaugurating the Christmas time of year that exhilarates her imagination and fuels the blaze of her heart, announces: 'It's fruitcake weather!'"

1 POUND BUTTER	2½ POUNDS CANDIED CHERRIES, HALVED
3 CUPS SUGAR	
12 LARGE EGGS	2 POUNDS CANDIED PINEAPPLE WEDGES
4 CUPS FLOUR	
2 TABLESPOONS ALLSPICE	1 POUND SLICED DATES
2 TABLESPOONS BAKING POWDER	½ POUND CHOPPED CANDIED ORANGE PEEL
¾ CUP PEACH BRANDY	2 POUNDS COARSELY CHOPPED PECANS

❄ Preheat oven to 325°F. Generously butter and flour six mini-loaf pans.
❄ With a mixer, cream butter and sugar.
❄ Add one egg at a time, beating each well.
❄ Sift the flour, allspice, and baking powder. Stir into the butter mixture with the brandy.
❄ Fold in the remaining ingredients, then spoon batter into pans, mounding the tops.
❄ Bake 1 hour and 15 minutes until tester comes out clean. Cool 15 minutes. Remove from pans and cool completely.

MAKES 6 MINI-FRUITCAKES

What is Christmas
But a shiver of hope—
That little leap of faith
Your heart takes
When you look into
The face of a child,
Let the day shine with joy,
With Love, and the dream of Peace.

LORD & TAYLOR

Let the children have their night of fun and laughter, let the gifts of Father Christmas delight their play. Let us grown-ups share to the full in their unstinted pleasures before we turn again to the stern tasks and the formidable years that lie before us, resolved that by our sacrifice and daring these same children shall not be robbed of their inheritance or denied their right to live in a free and decent world.

WINSTON CHURCHILL

"A Merry Christmas to us all, my dears. God bless us!" Which all the family re-echoed. "God bless us every one!" said Tiny Tim, the last of all.

CHARLES DICKENS

For somehow, not only at Christmas, but all the long year through, the joy that you give to others is the joy that comes back to you.

JOHN GREENLEAF WHITTIER

Joy to the world! The Lord is come:
    Let earth receive her King.
Let ev'ry heart prepare Him room,
    And heaven and nature sing,
    And heaven and nature sing,
    And heaven and heaven and nature sing.

ISAAC WATTS

"Glory to God in the highest, and on earth peace, good will toward men."

SAINT LUKE

O Christmas tree, O Christmas tree!
    How are thy leaves so verdant!
O Christmas tree, O Christmas tree
    How are thy leaves so verdant!

TRADITIONAL CAROL

The things we do at Christmas are touched with a certain extravagance, as beautiful, in some of its aspects, as the extravagance of Nature in June.

ROBERT COLLYER

Gingerbread Ornaments

*O*ur *Christmas tree
always seems more festive when hung with the
gingerbread ornaments we make each year.*

½ CUP BUTTER
6 TABLESPOONS SUGAR
¼ CUP BROWN SUGAR
½ CUP MOLASSES
1 EGG
2 CUPS FLOUR
1 TEASPOON BAKING
   POWDER

½ TEASPOON SALT
¼ TEASPOON BAKING SODA
2 TEASPOONS CINNAMON
1½ TEASPOONS GINGER
1 4-INCH TREE-SHAPED
   COOKIE CUTTER

❋ With an electric mixer, cream the butter with both sugars, molasses, and egg yolk.

❋ Mix the remaining ingredients, except the egg white, together. Stir into the butter mixture to form a stiff dough.

❋ Chill the dough 1 hour, then roll it out on a lightly floured surface to ⅛-inch thickness. Cut into tree shapes.

❋ Preheat oven to 350°F. and butter cookie sheets. Lift cookies onto the sheets and brush lightly with egg white.

❋ Bake 8 minutes until crisp. Make a hole 1 inch from the top of each cookie, then cool. Pipe edges with icing of your choice. Thread holes with gold cord.

MAKES 40 ORNAMENTS

Deep in the winter night, the family will come one by one, carrying great and small boxes, brilliant in all colors, ribboned in red and green, silver and gold, bright blue, placing them under me with the hands of their hearts, until all around me they are piled high, climbing up into my branches . . . the children in their pajamas and woolen slippers rub their sleeping eyes and stare at me in amazement. The mother with her hair hanging down her back smiles and glances here and there, and the father looks up and down at me, quiet and pleased . . . for I am the Christmas tree.

FRITZ PETERS

The holly and the ivy,
    When they are both full grown,
Of all the trees that are in the wood,
    The holly bears the crown.

TRADITIONAL CAROL

The Yule trees, and the dreams all children
    dream
The tremulous glow of candles in rows.
The gold and silver of angels and globes
And the splendor of tinsel and toys under trees.

BORIS PASTERNAK

Deck the halls with boughs of holly,
Fa la la la la, la la la la.
'Tis the season to be jolly,
Fa la la la la, la la la la.
Don we now our gay apparel,
Fa la la la la, la la la la.
Troll the ancient Yuletide carol,
Fa la la la la, la la la la.

WELSH CAROL

But give me holly,
Bold and jolly,
Honest, prickly,
Shining holly.
Pluck me holly
Leaf and berry
For the day when
I make merry.

CHRISTINA
ROSSETTI

My thoughts are drawn back, by a fascination which I do not care to resist, to my own childhood. I begin to consider, what do we all remember best upon the branches of the Christmas Tree of our own young Christmas days, by which we climbed to real life.

CHARLES DICKENS

A Glad Christmas

Old-Fashioned Eggnog

One of our happiest seasonal rituals is taking down our silver punch bowl and giving it a good polish. It actually takes longer than preparing this eggnog, which always brings a measure of good cheer to the festivities.

2 QUARTS PASTEURIZED EGGNOG, CHILLED
½ CUP LIGHT RUM
1 QUART VANILLA ICE CREAM, SOFTENED

2 CUPS HEAVY CREAM
½ CUP SUGAR
1 TABLESPOON VANILLA
1 TEASPOON NUTMEG

❄ Pour the eggnog into a punch bowl.
❄ Stir in the rum. (This recipe is still delicious without the rum, if desired.)
❄ Fold the ice cream into the eggnog until it is blended.
❄ In a separate large bowl, beat the heavy cream until frothy. Slowly add the sugar and vanilla, beating constantly until stiff.
❄ Gently fold the mixture into the eggnog.
❄ Sprinkle the nutmeg on top. Chill for 1 hour before serving.

MAKES 4 QUARTS OR 24 SERVINGS

The more the merrier.
JOHN HEYWOOD

This ancient silver bowl of mine, it tells of good
    old times,
Of joyous days and jolly nights, and merry
    Christmas times.

OLIVER WENDELL HOLMES

So now is come our joyful'st feast;
Let every man be jolly.
Each room with ivy leaves is dressed,
And every post with holly.
    Though some churls at our mirth repine
    Round your foreheads garlands twine,
    Drown sorrow in a cup of wine,
And let us all be merry.

GEORGE WITHER

On Christmas eve the bells were rung;
On Christmas eve the mass was sung:
That only night in all the year,
Saw the stoled priest the chalice rear.
The damsel donn'd her kirtle sheen;
The hall was dress'd with holly green,
Forth to the wood did merry-men go,
To gather in the mistletoe.

SIR WALTER SCOTT

Sitting under the mistletoe
(Pale green, fairy mistletoe)
One last candle burning low,
All the sleepy dancers gone,
Just one candle burning on,
Shadows lurking everywhere;
Someone came, and kissed me there.

WALTER DE LA MARE

Everywhere, everywhere,
Christmas tonight!

PHILLIPS BROOKS

I did not know she'd take it so,
    Or else I'd never dared;
Although the bliss was worth the blow,
    I did not know she'd take it so.
She stood beneath the mistletoe
    So long I thought she cared;
I did not know she'd take it so,
    Or else I'd never dared.

COUNTEE CULLEN

Christmas day. Lay pretty long in bed, and
then rose, leaving my wife desirous to sleep,
having sat up till four this morning seeing her
mayds make mince pies.

SAMUEL PEPYS

13

A
Joyful Christmas

Thumbprint Cookies

A*t Christmastime the kitchen becomes the center of our house. The children love making these cookies, and even the youngest can lend a thumb to help.*

1½ CUPS BUTTER
1½ CUPS SUGAR
2 EGG YOLKS
1 TABLESPOON GRATED ORANGE PEEL
1 TABLESPOON VANILLA

3 CUPS FLOUR
2 TEASPOONS BAKING POWDER
1 TEASPOON SALT
1 CUP RED RASPBERRY JAM

❄ With an electric mixer, cream the butter and sugar in a large bowl until light.

❄ Beat in the egg yolks, one at a time.

❄ Blend in the orange peel and vanilla.

❄ In another bowl, mix the flour, baking powder, and salt and stir into the butter mixture to make a soft dough. Chill 1 hour.

❄ Preheat oven to 350°F. and butter 2 cookie sheets.

❄ Using your fingers, shape the dough into 1-inch balls and place 1 inch apart on the cookie sheets. Make a thumb mark in each cookie.

❄ Bake 15 minutes until golden.

❄ Quickly top each cookie with ½ teaspoon jam, cool, then store in airtight tins.

MAKES 7 DOZEN COOKIES

Four angels standing on the four corners of the earth, holding the four winds of the earth.

REVELATION

Love came down at Christmas,
Love all lovely, love divine;
Love was born at Christmas,
Star and angels gave the sign.

CHRISTINA ROSSETTI

We shall rest! We shall hear the angels, we shall see the whole sky all diamonds . . . And our life will grow peaceful, tender, sweet as a caress. I believe, I do believe.

ANTON CHEKHOV

Be not forgetful to entertain strangers, for thereby some have entertained angels unawares.

SAINT PAUL

An angel writing in a book of gold.

LEIGH HUNT

O come all ye faithful,
    Joyful and triumphant,
O come ye, O come ye to Bethlehem.
    Come and behold Him,
Born the King of Angels!
    O come, let us adore Him,
    O come, let us adore Him,
    O come, let us adore Him,
        Christ the Lord.

ANCIENT CAROL

It is the stars,
The stars above us, govern our conditions.

WILLIAM SHAKESPEARE

Hark! the herald angels sing—
"Glory to the newborn King!
Peace on earth, and mercy mild,
God and sinners reconciled."
Joyful, all ye nations, rise,
Join the triumph of the skies;
With th' angelic host proclaim,
"Christ is born in Bethlehem."
Hark! the herald angels sing,
"Glory to the newborn King!"

CHARLES WESLEY

Best wishes for Xmas

Sweet Holiday Scones

There is an old carol that says, "I wish you a merry Christmas, 'tis good to be merry you know. I wish you a welcome reception, wherever to visit you go." Have these golden scones on hand for breakfast or afternoon tea, for unexpected guests.

2½ CUPS FLOUR
 1 TABLESPOON BAKING POWDER
 1 TEASPOON SALT
 ½ CUP COLD BUTTER
 ⅓ CUP SUGAR

 1 TEASPOON GRATED LEMON PEEL
 1 CUP CURRANTS (OPTIONAL)
 1 EGG
 ⅔ CUP MILK

❋ Preheat oven to 425°F. Butter 2 baking sheets.
❋ Mix flour, baking powder, and salt in a bowl. Add butter, breaking it into bits. Mix with the other ingredients.
❋ Mix in the sugar, lemon peel, and currants.
❋ In another bowl, whip the egg into the milk. Stir into the flour mixture until a ball forms.
❋ Using a spoon, drop 2-inch balls of the dough onto the baking sheets.
❋ Bake 12 minutes or until puffed and golden.
❋ Serve hot with sweetened whipped cream or butter and raspberry preserves.

MAKES 18 SCONES

I do hope your Christmas has had a little touch of Eternity in among the rush and pitter patter and all. It always seems such a mixing of this world and the next—but that after all is the idea!

EVELYN UNDERHILL

Heap on more wood!—the wind is chill;
But let it whistle as it will,
We'll keep our Christmas merry still.

SIR WALTER SCOTT

One dollar and eighty-seven cents. That was all. And sixty cents of it was in pennies. . . . Three times Della counted it. One dollar and eighty-seven cents. And the next day would be Christmas.

O. HENRY

How many observe Christ's birthday! How few, his precepts! O! 'tis easier to keep holidays than commandments.

BENJAMIN FRANKLIN

Success / four flights Thursday morning / all against twenty-one-mile wind / started from level with engine power alone / average speed through air thirty-one miles / longest fifty-nine seconds / inform press / home Christmas.

ORVILLE WRIGHT

20

I *am in a holiday humor.*
WILLIAM SHAKESPEARE

H*ow I wish we might be together these two Christmas days—I should so love to see you in the studio again. I have been working hard lately, just because of that Christmas sentiment, and because feeling is not enough: one must express it in one's work.*

VINCENT VAN GOGH

O *Christmas day, Oh! happy day,*
A foretaste from above,
To him who hath a happy home
And love returned from love!
SAMUEL TAYLOR COLERIDGE

M*ore things are wrought by prayer*
Than this world dreams of.
ALFRED, LORD TENNYSON

T*he holidays are welcome to me partly because they are such rallying points for the affections which get so much thrust aside in the business and preoccupations of daily life.*
GEORGE E. WOODBERRY

Best
Christmas
Wishes

English Trifle

I'll never forget the lovely Christmas we spent in London and the luscious trifle at the Connaught Hotel. Now I make my own creamy English trifle at home.

24 LADYFINGERS
⅔ CUP RASPBERRY JAM
⅓ CUP DRY SHERRY
3 PEARS
6 EGG YOLKS
½ CUP SUGAR

2 TABLESPOONS CORNSTARCH
2 CUPS SCALDED MILK
1 TABLESPOON VANILLA
1 CUP HEAVY CREAM
1 CUP SLICED TOASTED ALMONDS

❄ Split ladyfingers and spread both sides with jam. Line sides and bottom of a clear 3-quart bowl with them. Sprinkle with sherry.

❄ Poach, peel, and slice the pears. Set aside.

❄ Beat egg yolks with sugar and cornstarch until thick. Whisk in a saucepan with milk.

❄ Stir constantly over low heat about 5 minutes, until custard thickens. Cool 10 minutes, stir in vanilla, and refrigerate ½ an hour.

❄ Whip heavy cream until stiff and fold into the custard.

❄ Fill the bowl, layering the custard, pears, almonds, and any remaining ladyfingers. Chill.

MAKES 12 SERVINGS

In memory everything seems to happen to music.

TENNESSEE WILLIAMS

Jingle bells! Jingle bells! Jingle all the way!
Oh, what fun it is to ride in a one-horse open
    sleigh, hey!
Jingle bells! Jingle bells! Jingle all the way!
Oh, what fun it is to ride in a one-horse open
    sleigh, hey!

J. PIERPONT

I heard the bells on Christmas Day,
    Their old, familiar carols play,
        And wild and sweet
        The words repeat
    Of peace on earth, good-will to men!

HENRY WADSWORTH LONGFELLOW

Was there ever a wider and more loving
conspiracy than that which keeps the venerable
figure of Santa Claus from slipping away, with
all the other oldtime myths, into the forsaken
wonderland of the past?

HAMILTON WRIGHT MABIE

'Tis Christmas morning: Christmas mirth
And joyous voices fill the house.

THOMAS BAILEY ALDRICH

❄

Yesterday morning at a quarter of seven all the
children were up and dressed and began to
hammer at the door of their mother's and my
room, in which their six stockings, all bulging out
with queer angles and rotundities, were hanging
from the fireplace. . . . But first there was a
surprise . . . for Archie had a little Christmas
tree of his own which he had rigged up with the
help of one of the carpenters in a big closet; and
we all had to look at the tree and each of us got a
present off of it.

THEODORE ROOSEVELT

And he who gives a child a treat
Makes joy-bells ring in Heaven's street,
And he who gives a child a home
Builds palaces in Kingdom come.

JOHN MASEFIELD

These are the days that Reindeer love
And pranks the Northern Star.

EMILY DICKINSON

Christmas Greetings

Popcorn Balls

Place each popcorn ball in the center of a square of cellophane, twist, and tie with a pretty ribbon. Then pile them into a big bowl on a hall table for visiting friends to take home.

12 CUPS FRESHLY POPPED CORN
1 CUP UNSALTED PEANUTS
1 CUP RED CANDIED CHERRIES, QUARTERED
1½ CUPS LIGHT CORN SYRUP
½ CUP BROWN SUGAR
1 TABLESPOON VINEGAR
PINCH OF SALT
¼ CUP BUTTER

❄ Butter the inside of a bowl. Toss in the popped corn, peanuts, and cherries and mix well.
❄ Stir syrup, sugar, vinegar and salt in a saucepan over medium-high heat until it boils.
❄ Cook, without stirring, until a candy thermometer reaches 250°F. or a drop of syrup in cold water forms a hard ball.
❄ Remove pan from heat and stir in the butter.
❄ Pour syrup over corn mixture. Toss to coat.
❄ Butter your hands and, working very quickly, shape the mixture into 2-inch balls.

MAKES 16 POPCORN BALLS

The only things we ever keep
Are what we give away.

LOUIS GINSBERG

Christmas time and happy time,
  Set the bells to ringing.
Merry time and joyous time,
  Love its good gifts bringing.
Bright the way when love shines through,
  Short the way when hearts beat true;
Love will make all skies seem blue . . .
  Join the Yule-tide singing.

WILL M. MAUPIN

At Christmas play, and make good cheer,
For Christmas comes but once a year.

THOMAS TUSSER

So, God bless us, one and all,
With hearts and hearthstones warm,
And may he prosper great and small,
  And keep us out of harm;
  And teach us still His sweet good-will
This merry Christmas morning.

EDWIN WAUGH

28

Silent night, holy night!
   All is calm, all is bright.
Round yon Virgin, Mother and Child,
   Holy infant so tender and mild,
Sleep in heavenly peace,
   Sleep in heavenly peace.

JOSEPH MOHR

Were I a philosopher, I should write a
philosophy of toys, showing that nothing else in
life need be taken seriously, and that Christmas
Day in the company of children is one of the few
occasions on which men become entirely alive.

ROBERT LYND

Over the river and through the wood,
To grandfather's house we'll go;
   The horse knows the way
   To carry the sleigh,
Through the white and drifted snow.

LYDIA MARIA CHILD

Christmas won't be Christmas without any
presents.

LOUISA MAY ALCOTT

Sugarplums

These little treats, packed into pretty baskets, make a very nice teacher's present. Be sure to keep some to serve with ice cream or to tie onto the tree along with your gingerbread ornaments and popcorn garlands.

1 CUP DRIED APRICOTS	2 CUPS VANILLA WAFERS
1 CUP PECANS	1 CUP FLAKED COCONUT
½ CUP PITTED DATES	½ CUP ORANGE JUICE
½ CUP GOLDEN RAISINS	½ CUP SUGAR

❋ Finely chop the apricots, pecans, dates, and raisins in a food processor or with a sharp knife.
❋ Place several wafers in a plastic bag. Use a rolling pin to make 1 cup of crumbs.
❋ Place the fruit-and-nut mixture and the crumbs in a large bowl and toss with the coconut and orange juice.
❋ Using your fingers, form into ¾-inch balls. On a plate, roll the balls in sugar.
❋ Place in paper candy cups or wrap in little squares of clear cellophane, twist at the top, and tie with gold cord or narrow ribbon.

MAKES 5 DOZEN SUGARPLUMS

One doesn't forget the rounded wonder in the eyes of a boy as he comes bursting upstairs on Christmas morning and finds the two-wheeler or the fire truck of which for weeks he scarcely dared dream.

MAX LERNER

Christmas Eve, after I had hung my stocking, I lay awake a long time, pretending to be asleep and keeping alert to see what Santa Claus would do when he came.

HELEN KELLER

Our children await Christmas presents like politicians getting election returns; there's the Uncle Fred precinct and the Aunt Ruth district still to come in.

MARCELENE COX

The little toy dog is covered with dust, but
    sturdy and staunch he stands;
And the little toy soldier is covered with rust, and
    his musket moulds in his hands.
Time was when the little toy dog was new, and
    the soldier was passing fair;
And that was the time when our little boy blue
    kissed them and put them there.

EUGENE FIELD

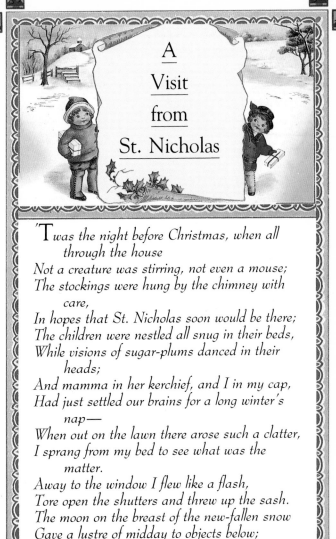

A Visit from St. Nicholas

'Twas the night before Christmas, when all
　　through the house
Not a creature was stirring, not even a mouse;
The stockings were hung by the chimney with
　　care,
In hopes that St. Nicholas soon would be there;
The children were nestled all snug in their beds,
While visions of sugar-plums danced in their
　　heads;
And mamma in her kerchief, and I in my cap,
Had just settled our brains for a long winter's
　　nap—
When out on the lawn there arose such a clatter,
I sprang from my bed to see what was the
　　matter.
Away to the window I flew like a flash,
Tore open the shutters and threw up the sash.
The moon on the breast of the new-fallen snow
Gave a lustre of midday to objects below;

When what to my wondering eyes should appear,
But a miniature sleigh and eight tiny reindeer,
With a little old driver, so lively and quick
I knew in a moment it must be St. Nick!
More rapid than eagles his coursers they came,
And he whistled and shouted, and called them
    by name:
"Now, Dasher! Now Dancer! Now, Prancer and
    Vixen!
On, Comet! On, Cupid! On, Donder and
    Blitzen!
To the top of the porch, to the top of the wall!
Now dash away, dash away, dash away all!"
As dry leaves that before the wild hurricane fly,
When they meet with an obstacle, mount to the
    sky,
So up to the house-top the coursers they flew,
With the sleigh full of toys—and St. Nicholas,
    too.
And then in a twinkling I heard on the roof
The prancing and pawing of each little hoof.
As I drew in my head, and turning around,
Down the chimney St. Nicholas came with a
    bound.
He was dressed all in fur from his head to his
    foot,
And his clothes were all tarnished with ashes
    and soot;
A bundle of toys he had flung on his back,
And he looked like a peddler just opening his
    pack.

His eyes, how they twinkled! His dimples, how
merry!
His cheeks were like roses, his nose like a cherry;
His droll little mouth was drawn up like a bow,
And the beard on his chin was as white as the
snow.
The stump of a pipe he held tight in his teeth,
And the smoke it encircled his head like a
wreath.
He had a broad face and a little round belly
That shook, when he laughed, like a bowl full of
jelly.
He was chubby and plump—a right jolly old elf;
And I laughed, when I saw him, in spite of
myself.
A wink of his eye and a twist of his head
Soon gave me to know I had nothing to dread.
He spoke not a word, but went straight to his
work,
And filled all the stockings; then turned with a
jerk,
And laying his finger aside of his nose,
And giving a nod, up the chimney he rose.
He sprang in his sleigh, to his team gave a
whistle,
And away they all flew like the down of a thistle;
But I heard him exclaim, ere he drove out of
sight:
"Happy Christmas to all, and to all a good-
night!"

CLEMENT C. MOORE

The hour was now midnight and quite a bit
   past,
But our labors, thank Heaven, were finished at
   last . . .
As we gazed at our efforts through lead-lidded
   eyes
And thought of the morrow and shouts of
   surprise,
We prayed that the children, the morn of St.
   Nick's
Would please not awaken at least until six!

RICHARD ARMOUR

Jo was the first to wake in the gray dawn of
Christmas morning. No stockings hung at the
fireplace, and for a moment she felt as much
disappointed as she did long ago, when her little
sock fell down because it was so crammed with
goodies. Then she remembered her mother's
promise, and slipping her hand under her pillow,
drew out a little crimson-covered book.

LOUISA MAY ALCOTT

Hear the sledges with the bells—
      Silver bells!
What a world of merriment their melody foretells!
   How they tinkle, tinkle, tinkle,
      In the icy air of night!

EDGAR ALLAN POE

The Christmas bells from hill to hill
    Answer each other in the mist.

ALFRED, LORD TENNYSON

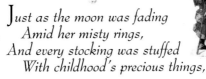

Just as the moon was fading
    Amid her misty rings,
And every stocking was stuffed
    With childhood's precious things,

Old Kriss Kringle looked round,
    And saw on the elm-tree bough,
High-hung, an oriole's nest,
    Silent and empty now.

"Quite like a stocking," he laughed,
    "Pinned up there on the tree!
Little I thought the birds
    Expected a present from me!"

Then old Kriss Kringle, who loves
    A joke as well as the best,
Dropped a handful of flakes
    In the oriole's empty nest.

THOMAS BAILEY ALDRICH

'Most all the time, the whole year round, there
    ain't no flies on me,
But jest 'fore Christmas I'm as good as I kin be!

EUGENE FIELD

Kindest Greetings for Christmas

Christmas Morn Popovers

C*harles Dickens wrote,*
"Christmas Day should be fragrant with the love
that we bear one another." It should also be
fragrant with fresh baking. These special
popovers, and the smiling faces I see around the
table, mean Christmas morning to me.

6 EGGS
6 TABLESPOONS MELTED
  BUTTER
1 CUP HEAVY CREAM

1 CUP MILK
2 CUPS FLOUR
1 TEASPOON SALT
¼ TEASPOON NUTMEG

❄ Preheat oven to 400°F. Butter muffin tins.
❄ With an electric mixer, beat the eggs until
frothy, then add the butter, cream, and milk.
❄ In a separate bowl, stir flour, salt, and
nutmeg. Beat into the egg mixture *just* until
smooth.
❄ Spoon into muffin cups until ¾ full.
❄ Bake for 35 minutes, until golden.
❄ To keep puffy, quickly make a tiny slit in
the top of each popover to let the steam escape.
❄ Remove the popovers from tins and serve.

MAKES 18 POPOVERS

It's food too fine for angels; yet come, take
And eat thy fill! It's Heaven's sugar cake.

EDWARD TAYLOR

Sing a song of mincemeat,
Currants, raisins, spice,
Apples, sugar, nutmeg,
Every thing that's nice,
Stir it with a ladle,
Wish a lovely wish,
Drop it in the middle
Of your well-filled dish,
Stir again for good luck,
Pack it all away
Tied in little jars and pots,
Until Christmas Day.

ELIZABETH GOULD

Never did Christmas board display a more
goodly and gracious assemblage of countenances;
those who were not handsome were, at least,
happy; and happiness is a rare improver of your
hard-favoured visage.

WASHINGTON IRVING

40

Christmas is coming, the geese are getting fat,
Please to put a penny in the old man's hat;
If you haven't got a penny, a ha'penny will do,
If you haven't got a ha'penny, God bless you.

OLD ENGLISH CAROL

"I think it must be the field-mice," replied the
Mole. . . . "They go round carol-singing regularly
at this time of the year. They're quite an
institution in these parts. And they never pass
me over—they come to Mole End last of all; and
I used to give them hot drinks, and supper too
sometimes, when I could afford it."

KENNETH GRAHAME

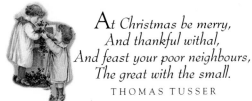

At Christmas be merry,
And thankful withal,
And feast your poor neighbours,
The great with the small.

THOMAS TUSSER

Mary and Laura pulled out two small packages.
They unwrapped them, and each found a little
heart-shaped cake. Over their delicate brown tops
was sprinkled white sugar. The sparkling grains
lay like tiny drifts of snow.

LAURA INGALLS WILDER

ALL HAPPINESS AT
CHRISTMAS-TIDE.

The riches of a
happy heart
And all the best
that life
can give.
That Best
I wish for you.

Fresh Cranberry Chutney

This delicious relish complements turkey, goose, or ham. It is a welcome hostess gift, especially since it turns inevitable leftovers into tasty snacks.

1 RED APPLE, UNPEELED
1 ORANGE, UNPEELED
1 CUP SEEDLESS GRAPES
1 POUND CRANBERRIES
1½ CUPS SUGAR
1 CUP CRANBERRY JUICE
½ CUP ORANGE JUICE

⅓ CUP CIDER VINEGAR
1 TEASPOON ALLSPICE
3 CINNAMON STICKS
1½ CUPS WALNUTS, CHOPPED
1 CUP COCKTAIL ONIONS, DRAINED

❄ Cube the apple; seed and chop the orange; quarter the grapes, and set aside.

❄ Wash the cranberries, remove stems, and place in a saucepan. Stir in sugar, cranberry juice, orange juice, vinegar, allspice, and cinnamon sticks.

❄ Bring to a full boil over medium-high heat. Reduce heat and cook 15 minutes or until berries pop.

❄ Add the fruits, nuts, and onions. Cook over low heat, stirring occasionally, until mixture thickens (about 30 minutes).

❄ Discard the cinnamon sticks and cool. Can be refrigerated up to 2 weeks. Serve cold.

MAKES 1½ QUARTS

Scanning the heavens I am reminded of another star from long ago.

GALILEO GALILEI

The good things in life are not to be had singly, but come to us with a mixture.

CHARLES LAMB

As the purse is emptied the heart is filled.

VICTOR HUGO

A good conscience is a continual Christmas.

BENJAMIN FRANKLIN

Not what we give, but what we share,
For the gift without the giver is bare;
Who gives himself with his alms feeds three.
Himself, his hungering neighbor, and me.

JAMES RUSSELL LOWELL

He who waits to do a great deal of good at once, will never do anything.

SAMUEL JOHNSON

No act of kindness, no matter how small, is ever wasted.

AESOP

On the twelfth day of Christmas
My true love sent to me
Twelve lords a-leaping,
Eleven ladies dancing,
Ten pipers piping,
Nine drummers drumming,
Eight maids a-milking,
Seven swans a-swimming,
Six geese a-laying,
Five golden rings,
Four colly birds,
Three French hens,
Two turtle-doves
And a partridge in a pear-tree.

TRADITIONAL CAROL

It is not the weight of jewel or plate,
    Or the fondle of silk or fur;
'Tis the spirit in which the gift is rich,
    As the gifts of the Wise Ones were,
And we are not told whose gift was gold,
    Or whose was the gift of myrrh.

EDMUND VANCE COOKE

45

A Merry Christmas

Star Sugar Cookies

*These cookies make a
tasty gift and travel well to out-of-town relatives
and faraway friends. Pack them in wax paper
and tuck into colorful tins.*

1 CUP BUTTER	⅓ CUP MILK
1 CUP SUGAR	2 TABLESPOONS VANILLA
2 EGGS	1 TABLESPOON GRATED
3½ CUPS FLOUR	LEMON PEEL
1 TABLESPOON BAKING	STAR COOKIE CUTTER
POWDER	GREEN AND RED
¼ TEASPOON SALT	CANDIED CHERRIES

❋ With an electric mixer, cream the butter,
sugar, and eggs.
❋ In another bowl, mix flour, baking powder,
and salt, and stir into butter mixture with
the milk. Blend in vanilla and lemon peel.
❋ Chill the dough 1 hour, then roll it onto a
lightly floured surface to ⅛-inch thickness.
❋ Heat oven to 400°F. and butter 2 cookie
sheets.
❋ Cut the dough into stars. Lift the cookies
onto the sheets. Decorate each with half a
candied cherry. Bake about 8 minutes or until
lightly browned. Remove to racks to cool.

MAKES 8 DOZEN COOKIES

How pretty it is to watch the tiny flakes drift downward through the air as if there were a wedding in the sky and the fairies were throwing confetti.

CYRIL W. BEAUMONT

Summer fading, winter comes—
Frosty mornings, tingling thumbs,
Window robins, winter rooks,
And the picture story-books.

ROBERT LOUIS STEVENSON

The first fall of snow is not only an event but it is a magical event. You go to bed in one kind of a world and wake up to find yourself in another quite different, and if this is not enchantment, then where is it to be found?

J. B. PRIESTLEY

For, creeping softly underneath
　　The door when all the lights are out,
Jack Frost takes every breath you breathe,
　　And knows the things you think about.

GABRIEL SETOUN

No cloud above, no earth below
A universe of sky and snow.
JOHN GREENLEAF WHITTIER

If Winter comes, can Spring be far behind?
PERCY BYSSHE SHELLEY

Words like winter snowflakes.
HOMER

The frolic architecture of the snow.
RALPH WALDO EMERSON

"I have often thought," says Sir Roger, "it happens well that Christmas should fall out in the middle of winter."
JOSEPH ADDISON

Silent, and soft, and slow
Descends the snow.
HENRY WADSWORTH LONGFELLOW

Let us love winter, for it is the spring of genius.
PIETRO ARETINO

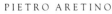

A Jolly Christmas

Pumpkin Pie

"What calls back the past, like the rich pumpkin pie?" said John Greenleaf Whittier. The fun of holiday baking brings back my own holiday memories.

3 EGGS
1 CAN (16 OZ.) SOLID-PACK PUMPKIN
1 CUP BROWN SUGAR
2 TEASPOONS CINNAMON
½ TEASPOON GINGER
½ TEASPOON NUTMEG
¼ TEASPOON CLOVES

PINCH OF SALT
1 CUP LIGHT CREAM
½ CUP EVAPORATED MILK
1 TABLESPOON MAPLE SYRUP
1 UNBAKED 9-INCH FLAKY PIE CRUST

❄ Preheat oven to 425°F.
❄ With an electric mixer, beat the eggs in a large bowl until light yellow.
❄ Stir in the pumpkin, sugar, cinnamon, ginger, nutmeg, cloves, and salt until smooth.
❄ Blend in the cream, milk, and maple syrup.
❄ Pour into the unbaked crust.
❄ Bake 15 minutes. Reduce heat to 350°F. and bake 45 minutes or until filling rises and sets.

MAKES 1 PIE OR ABOUT 8 SERVINGS

On the approach of a New Year, we, too, can believe in something better than experience has justified us in hoping for.

ROBERT LYND

A Flower unblown: a Book unread:
A Tree with fruit unharvested:
A Path untrod: a House whose rooms
Lack yet the heart's divine perfumes:
This is the Year that for you waits
Beyond Tomorrow's mystic gates.

HORATIO NELSON POWERS

Ring out the old, ring in the new,
Ring, happy bells, across the snow:
The year is going, let him go;
Ring out the false, ring in the true.

ALFRED, LORD TENNYSON

Now the New Year reviving old Desires,
The thoughtful Soul to Solitude retires.

OMAR KHAYYAM

Be at War with your Vices, at Peace with your Neighbours, and let every New Year find you a better Man.

BENJAMIN FRANKLIN

We wish you a Merry Christmas,
We wish you a Merry Christmas,
We wish you a Merry Christmas,
  And a Happy New Year.

TRADITIONAL CAROL

Here we come a-wassailing
  Among the leaves so green,
Here we come a wand'ring,
  So fair to be seen.
Love and joy come to you,
  And to you your wassail too,
And God bless you and send you a happy
  new year,
And God send you a happy new year.

ENGLISH CAROL

Many merry Christmases, many happy New Years. Unbroken friendships, great accumulations of cheerful recollections and affections on earth, and heaven for us all.

CHARLES DICKENS

A Happy
new Year

Festive Wassail Punch

W*inter means clear, crisp, sunny afternoons spent ice skating or sledding. Afterward, nothing is cozier than a traditional bowl of warm punch, surrounded by holly leaves.*

1 CUP WATER	2 CINNAMON STICKS
2 CUPS SUGAR	2 CUPS DRY SHERRY
1 TEASPOON NUTMEG	½ CUP BRANDY
1 TEASPOON GINGER	6 EGGS
12 WHOLE CLOVES	1 ORANGE

❄ Boil water and sugar over high heat.
❄ Reduce heat, add nutmeg, ginger, cloves, cinnamon sticks, sherry, and brandy. Simmer for 10 minutes. Remove from heat.
❄ Discard cloves and cinnamon sticks.
❄ With an electric mixer, beat the egg yolks on high speed until thick and lemon colored.
❄ Whisk the yolks into the hot spiced mixture and stir constantly over low heat for 5 minutes.
❄ Pour into a heat-proof punch bowl.
❄ Beat the egg whites until stiff, and spoon gently on top of the wassail punch.
❄ Garnish with thin orange slices. Serve hot.

MAKES 1 ½ QUARTS OR 12 SERVINGS

As evening drew on, hearts beat fast with anticipation, hands were full of ready gifts. There were the tremulously expectant words of the church service, the night was past and the morning was come, the gifts were given and received, joy and peace made a flapping of wings in each heart, there was a great burst of carols, the Peace of the World had dawned, strife had passed away, every hand was linked in hand, every heart was singing.

D. H. LAWRENCE

Should auld acquaintance be forgot,
And never brought to mind?
Should auld acquaintance be forgot,
And auld lang syne!
For auld lang syne, my dear,
For auld lang syne,
We'll tak a cup o' kindness yet
For auld lang syne!

ROBERT BURNS